NON-RESISTANCE AS A POLICE FORCE.

THE object of this tract is to show the practical application of Non-Resistance principles to the treatment of criminals: to show that those laws upon which the good order and welfare of the community depend might be more efficiently enforced by the hands of Non-Resistants, and in conformity with their ideas, than as now administered: and to show that, under such a system, a constant and progressive diminution of all sorts of crime may reasonably be expected.

Non-Resistance is as yet unknown to the community, except by its negative side. By saying this, I do not mean to imply that even its negative side is clearly understood by the mass of those who criticise it. Their judgment of it is usually formed by hearing the bare statement (commonly passing through the minds and mouths of its enemies) that Non-Resistance is a mere renunciation of all the means at present used for protection against evil-doers, without the attempt to substitute any thing in their place; that it is the discharge of constables, judges and juries, the pulling down of jails, the dismantling of forts and frigates, and the disbanding of army and navy; that it is disregard of law, and contempt of authority; that it is a license to ruffians to work their will upon the persons and property of the community; that it is a man's standing still to see the butchery of his wife and children; that it implies passive submission to all sorts of injury, without the attempt either to repel it or to preserve one's self from it; that it involves the entire surrender of all rights, public and private, to whomsoever is pleased to invade them; that it is a "no-government system"; that it would leave virtue and industry defenceless, and offer perfect success and perfect impunity to the enterprises of ambition, avarice and lust. This is the portrait of Non-Resistance given to the public by the periodical press; the "*religious*" portion of it usually adding the statement that Non-Resistance is identified with, or nearly allied to, Infidelity.

It is not strange, then, that practical, business men, that sensible women, receiving this account from those whom they suppose to speak intelligently and truly, should assume the Non-Resistants to be fanatics, and their scheme an absurdity, and turn from both with indifference, or contempt, or abhorrence, according to the point of view from which each person regards them.

The object of these pages is, while giving some aid towards the formation of a correct public opinion upon these points, to show that Non-Resistance may be efficiently applied to the defence of a community against internal dangers; that it may operate successfully as a police force.

Non-Resistance objects, not to government, but to an anti-Christian mode of governing; not to physical force, but to injurious force; not to the restraint of malefactors, but to a system which contents itself with punishing, without attempting, or wishing, to reform them. It objects, in short, only to violations of the Golden Rule.

War is a combination of many evils. It confounds the innocent with the guilty, and practises robbery and murder alike upon both. It wastes human life, depraves morals, destroys the products of industry, and discourages all the labors of peaceful life; but its great, its radical vice is, that it seems to give the sanction of legitimate authority to the practice of overcoming evil with evil. It publishes to the world, as a right and just mode of procedure, that, because our neighbor has done us a wrong, we may and will do him one, and if possible, a greater. It does not, in the least, recognize the Christian principle of overcoming evil with good.

The practice of judicial murder, commonly called capital punishment, that formal elaboration of lynch law which gives it an outward conformity to the manners and customs of civilized life, is a combination of many evils. By it, the State gives an example to the individual of violating the sacredness of human life; by it the anti-Christian doctrine of retaliation is officially and effectually taught; and by it a human being, often a grossly vicious one, is violently thrust out of the position in which his Maker placed him, has his course of reformatory discipline (as far as this world is concerned) prematurely cut short by unauthorized hands, and is prevented from making that reparation for his offences which subsequent reformation might have disposed him to make. But the radical vice of this custom also is, that it seems to give the sanction of legitimate authority to the practice of overcoming evil with evil.

The penalty of imprisonment for crime, as now practised, involves many evils. It places the criminal in a position, and under influences, which, if he is not already hardened to the utmost extent, are likely to make him worse instead of better. It deprives his wife and children of such care and support as he gave them, without attempting, or caring, to make for their bodies and souls such provision as their welfare, and the welfare of the State, alike demand; and it entirely disregards the fact that a large proportion of discharged convicts are worse men, more likely to repeat their crimes, and more dangerous to the well-being of society when they come out, than when they went in. But the radical vice of this, as of the other customs I have instanced, is that it seems to give the sanction of legitimate authority to the practice of overcoming evil with evil. It neither recognizes the brotherhood of individual men, nor provides, by other than the coarsest temporary make-shifts, for the welfare of the community.

The Non-Resistants, as I have said, are not no-government men. But they are not satisfied with a government which attempts to fulfil only half, and the poorer half, of its proper function, and accomplishes that half by unchristian means. They wish to see a higher purpose pursued, and better means used to effect it.

It is, then, a natural, and a not altogether unreasonable request, for those who have listened patiently to the complaints of the Non-Resistants to reply, "Give us *your* plan. Our present system has been formed by the accumulation of the thoughts and labor of our wisest men, devoted for centuries to this object. Our legislators have done what they could, and, as we think, not without a good measure of success, to embody wisdom and justice in our code of laws; but if you are dissatisfied with their labors, give us your better system; show us the plan that shall protect the community from its vicious members as thoroughly as ours does, and shall at the same time accomplish what *you* think necessary for the welfare and reformation of the malefactors and their families. Prove to us that your system is really better, and you need not fear but it will be adopted."

This demand, I say, is not altogether unreasonable; but it is not altogether reasonable.

When a great system has been for centuries in steady operation, recognized and accepted by a whole nation as their chief rule of action, and really contributing very much to their comfort and convenience in some particulars, it cannot be superseded, even by a better, without some temporary inconvenience and discomfort. However plain it may be that I need a better house, and how much better soever may be the new one, the process of removal is always a sacrifice of comfort and convenience, for the time; and even some of the improvements of the new house will seem unsatisfactory, until use has habituated us to them. To be turned out of our accustomed course, even into a better, is at first an annoyance.

But the difficulty of accepting any plan which the Non-Resistants may offer is still further enhanced by the fact that the external convenience of the community is not its chief object, and that it may not at first, perhaps, secure that end so thoroughly as the present system does.

Welfare is sometimes a very different thing from convenience, and is then to be attained by very different means. To give a troublesome child a box on the ear may be the speediest way of relieving yourself from present annoyance; but it is not therefore the *best* way, either of accomplishing this purpose, or fulfilling your duty to the child.

In commencing any undertaking, our purpose and effort should be twofold; to do the right thing, and to do it in the right manner. But in the matter of criminal jurisprudence, we have not yet even attempted either of these, if the Christian* system is admitted to be our proper guide. The object of our penal system is to protect the community by inflicting such vengeance on the transgressor as shall tend to deter him and others from doing the like again, and in effecting this, we not only directly violate the Christian rule of forgiveness of enemies, but we put the bad man into a position whose tendency is to make him worse. The whole proceeding is as selfish as that of the baker who puts up the price of bread when the people are starving; and like all selfishness, it creates more harm than it cures; it palliates the symptoms, but confirms the disease.

The purpose of a well-ordered community will be the welfare of ALL; of the minority as well as of the majority; and none the less when the minority is a minority of one, and that one the worst person in the community. The greater the need, material or spiritual, the greater the obligation resting upon those who can supply that need; and if there be a poverty so extensive, a wickedness so desperate, as to be invincible save by the efforts and resources of the whole community, the removal of that poverty or wickedness should be considered as the very purpose for which God gave to the community strength and wealth, mind and conscience.

* The words *Christian* and *Christianity* have been so extensively and so variously misused by sectarians, and are so generally misapplied in common speech and writing — the word Christian being used as if it meant merely church-member, and Christianity being held to include those things (and no more) which cause a man to be admitted to church-membership — that I must define the sense in which I use them.

By Christianity, I mean the rule of living which Jesus of Nazareth summed up in these two provisions — TO LOVE GOD WITH THE WHOLE HEART, AND OUR NEIGHBOR AS OURSELVES; defining our neighbor to be any one who is in need that we can relieve, without regard to color, creed, country or condition — illustrating the nature of love by showing that it should be *practical* in its operation, and should include even our enemies — further explaining that this love must have a constant and active energy in reforming the world, *overcoming* its evil, and overcoming it *with good* — and emphatically enjoining that all good shall be cherished and all evil overcome in each man's own heart and life, as well as in the world around him.

This rule of living is what I mean by Christianity; I hold it to be the *right* rule; and I so decide because it is the *best* I can find, or conceive of. It seems to me perfect, adapted in the most thorough manner to secure the progressive improvement, the welfare, and thus the happiness, of the human race. And the life which constantly strives for conformity to it, I call a *Christian* life.

The Christian idea of government includes this, that it shall be administered equally for the benefit of ALL; that it shall regard and promote the welfare of the weakest, the poorest, and the worst man in the community, equally with that of the strongest, richest and best. The weakest most needs help, and should therefore receive it from the combined strength, prompted by the combined goodness, and directed by the combined wisdom, of the community, not doing for him, but helping him to do for himself, all that is needful. In like manner, the poorest should be assisted by the combined wealth, goodness and wisdom of the community, not to make him rich by giving, but to explore for him the causes of poverty, and give him instruction and help to overcome them. Thus also the most depraved and perverse should be assisted by the combined patience, wisdom and goodness of the community, in the point where *his* necessity is greatest, namely, in attaining the power of self-control, and the disposition to exert it, with what else remains of a true mental, moral and religious culture.

But here an obvious difficulty arises. You can help the weak who wishes for strength, and the poor man who is struggling to rise above poverty, but how are you to help the vicious man who rejoices in his depravity and rejects with scorn your offer of the means of improvement? Is he to be helped against his will, and by infringement of his natural liberty?

I answer, if his violations of the rights of others prove too great for patience to bear, and too obstinate for love and the return of good for evil to overcome, after these methods have been fairly and fully tried, he *is* to be helped against his will, and deprived of that liberty which experience has shown him determined to abuse. But this course must not be the abandonment of patience and love, but a prolongation of them under a new form. The offender's own welfare is no more to be lost sight of in restraining him from the opportunity of theft, or drunkenness, or murder, than the welfare of a child is lost sight of by the wise parent who separates him from the brothers with whom he persists in quarrelling. The remedy should be not less suited to the real needs of the offending than of the suffering party; and it should be so obviously dictated by real benevolence, so plainly designed as well as suited, and suited as well as designed, to promote the offender's welfare, that he himself shall see this and be grateful for it, whenever he returns to his right mind.

Here, then, is the problem before us: how to combine an adequate amount of protection to the community (an amount ultimately as great or greater than is attained by our present penal system) with a Christian regard to the rights, the necessities, in one word, to the *welfare* of our fellow-sinner whose vices call for restraint and correction. Is it possible to do this; and, if possible, *how* is it to be done? This is the question asked by the community of the Non-Resistants, in answer to their criticisms on the existing method.

The Non-Resistants reply — We claim neither a monopoly of wisdom, nor a peculiar fitness for the legislative function. We are aware that the formation of a wise code of laws, and of the apparatus needful for the administration thereof, far from being a simple or an easy thing, requires a long and careful exercise of the best theoretical and practical wisdom of the nation. Our first contribution (no slight or unimportant one,) to the amendment of American legislation has already been made; namely, the pointing out, in the lectures, discussions, and tracts of our Society, that the fundamental dogma, and many of the special provisions of American legislation, are at variance with the Christian system. We have shown that not the will of the majority, but the will of God, is the supreme law of the land; that when human laws contradict the obvious rules of right and justice, they can impose no obligation upon the citizen, but are null and void from the beginning, and should be treated as such by all who would obey God rather than men; and that we need a legislative and executive system which shall recognize, and be founded on, and be thoroughly conformed to, these ideas of right and justice, as they are interpreted by the Christian system.

Many persons who agree with Carlyle in nothing else, join him in sneering at the modern efforts of philanthropy as "sickly humanity and rose-pink sentimentalism." But however they may ridicule the motive, all must agree, that if the ends proposed by the Non-Resistants are feasible, their accomplishment is very much to be desired. If society can really be better protected from the depredations of the vicious without hanging and severe imprisonment than with them, if malefactors can really be changed from bad men to good by a discipline different from the present during their period of restraint, all will agree that these changes are desirable. But the question still recurs — How are they to be effected?

How are other great objects of public interest effected? When an abundant supply of pure water is needed in Boston — when increased facilities for the education of children and of teachers are required — when an improved postal system is thought desirable — when the necessities of mankind demand a speedier mode of travelling, and a lightning-like rapidity in the transmission of intelligence to distant places — how do men act? Do they assume that the yet unattained good is an impossibility, and that any plan for its attainment must be chimerical? Not at all! They set the most hearty enthusiasm, the largest experience, the best theoretical and practical wisdom of the city or the State at work upon the problem, and persevere through all sorts of discouragement and difficulty to its accomplishment; and through such means we have seen these very improvements made within the past twenty-five years.

We ask only that the same methods may be used to effect the improvement of our penal legislation, which have been successfully applied to so many other subjects. Our present treatment of criminals is at variance with that Christianity by which we have named ourselves, and which we assume to be the perfect rule of life. Let the best wisdom and the highest skill of the State be put in requisition, to place our laws, and the administration of them, in accordance with our religion. Let it be given in charge to men combining the loftiest intellectual powers with a just estimate of the predominant claims of morality and religion, to make a deliberate and thorough examination of the subject, and report a plan whereby this purpose may be effected. And let the people, by public and private discussion of the various rights, duties and interests combined in the great subject above mentioned, prepare themselves for intelligent action upon this plan, when it shall be matured.

We need not discard an iota of the true wisdom which has been incorporated into our Constitution and laws; but wherever right has been postponed to a supposed expediency, wherever justice has been so construed as to conflict with love, wherever the claim of the magistrate has sought to invalidate the supremacy of the Creator, reform is demanded, and demanded by our interest not less than by our duty.

Much of the sagacity which has exerted itself in legislation has been misapplied and wasted by acting on the false principle above named, that the will of the people is the supreme law of the land. But the same skill, building on a firmer foundation, the supremacy of right and justice, can of course erect a more useful and durable structure. We only ask that the efforts of the State may be put forth in this direction, and that our Constitution and laws may be so reörganized that our duty as Christians shall no longer conflict with the claim made upon us as citizens; that it may become possible for us to honor and obey the civil ruler, without forfeiting our allegiance to the King of Kings.

The Christian system accomplishes the welfare of man more thoroughly than any other; but it attains this end only through an extended process of self-discipline, which first prompts its subjects to strive to do right because it is their duty, and as fast as they reduce this duty to practice, shows them that their truest interest, their highest welfare and happiness, are secured by this very allegiance to duty. But before this self-discipline has been attained, while men are seeking happiness with eyes unenlightened by a sense of the supremacy of duty, the requisitions of Christianity sometimes seem directly opposed to their happiness, and hence are disregarded. The miser, who knows no higher pleasure than hoarding his money, shrinks from the precept, "Give to him that asketh thee," and feels a pang for every penny that he bestows; it is not until he has discerned and begun to practise the duty of liberality, that he finds the enjoyment of giving to be far greater than that of hoarding. The Turk, who thinks three wives better than one, and the civilized voluptuary who prefers a concubine to a wife, reject the divine law of marriage as a restriction on their pleasures; ignorant that the blessed sacrament by which two well-adapted souls and bodies are mingled in one, and pledged permanently and solely to each other, confers a lasting and constantly increasing delight, far above their highest momentary enjoyments. In like manner the men and the nations which have hitherto contented themselves with applying to malefactors the system of judicial retaliation commonly and erroneously called "justice," are alarmed at the very idea of no longer taking an eye for an eye, a tooth for a tooth, and life for life, and cry out that the very foundations of society are subverted when it is proposed to treat these malefactors by the Christian method of returning good for evil. They do not see that patiently to suffer curses and buffetings, violence and robbery, and return them with blessings and benefactions, suited to soften the heart of the evil-doer, are as honorable in a merchant as in a missionary, in a mechanic of the present day as in a saint or martyr of apostolic times; and that this course is far better fitted than their present one, not only to honor Christ and benefit the souls of men, but to rear a secure and perfect social structure! They do not see that the adoption of the Christian method of overcoming evil with good, and a voluntary acceptance of the temporary evils of a change of system, would ultimately insure to them not only a far higher measure of security than they now enjoy, but a decrease, in geometrical ratio, in every department of crime.

The purposes to be accomplished are these: —

I.

To have, as the basis of legislative, judicial and executive action, a Constitution founded upon justice and righteousness.

II.

To have a code of laws so strictly in conformity with the Divine law of love that, while aiming equally to secure the welfare of all, they shall take special care not to overlook the necessities of the poorest, or the weakest, or the worst member of the community.

III.

To have not only the laws, but the apparatus for executing them, and every stage and process in the system by which they are enforced, in perfect conformity with the law of love; namely: to have all those persons, from the highest to the lowest, who are charged with the maintenance of good order in the community, namely, police officers, sheriffs, constables, and jailers, as well as judges, chosen from among those most highly gifted with intelligence, integrity, humanity, acuteness in the discernment of character, and tact and skill to conduct the various relations which they are to hold with criminals in the manner best suited to promote *their permanent welfare*, which will of course also, as far as they are concerned, be the best means of promoting the welfare of the community.

IV.

To have the penal laws always contemplate, as one of their chief objects, the *reformation* of the criminal, and to have all their provisions *designed* and *suited* to promote his true welfare, and prepare him for a return to society whenever the improvement of his character shall seem to authorize it.

I take it for granted that most persons will admit the objects sketched above to be desirable, and the majority of them to be feasible. Thus it is obvious, that if the people cared for such things, and were disposed to take the trouble, they could frame a Constitution which should recognize Right and Justice as the supreme law, to which, not less indispensably than to the "will of the people," all specific statutes should be conformed; that they could assume and establish the natural right of the *whole* people to liberty, instead of merely five-sixths of them; that they could establish "Reform Schools" for men and women *convicted* of crime, as well as for boys and girls commencing the course which tends in that direction; that they could use the public resources as thoroughly in subjecting such persons to a reformatory discipline, and persevere in that work as assiduously as they now do in the inferior one of merely *punishing* malefactors; and that by suitably honoring and recompensing those who take charge of this most important branch of the public welfare, they could attract to it the needed qualifications, namely, the very highest learning, wisdom, experience, intellect and moral power which the nation affords.

But to those whose thoughts have not previously taken this particular direction, it is *not* so obvious how the penal department of the government can be administered without disregarding, temporarily, at least, the welfare of the malefactor.

He is assumed to have forfeited all his rights by crime, and is disposed of solely as the welfare of the community is supposed to require. When the warrant for his apprehension is issued, it is to be executed at all hazards, even though his life should be sacrificed in the attempt, and his effort to escape while under restraint is resisted to the same extremity. If the safety of the community is assumed to require the sacrifice of his life, he is deliberately killed by officers of the law, with solemn judicial and clerical formalities, regardless not only of his "inalienable" right to life, but of the claims which wife, children, relatives or friends may have upon him. Even those who allow that he still has rights do not see how these can be practically conceded to him without a sacrifice of the rights, and welfare, and safety of the community; and the doubter who has been compelled to admit that a criminal, once secured in the possession of the community, may be kept subjected to solely beneficent influences until it shall appear safe to release him, will still insist that the act of arresting an armed and violent man must necessarily be performed with arms and violence, regardless of any injuries that he may suffer in the attempt. I shall try to show that this idea is unfounded, that justice may be executed upon a criminal without the infliction of injury, that the community may be protected without disregarding the rights even of an offender, and that the policeman and the constable may overcome evil, not with evil, but with good.

To test the correctness of these ideas, let us apply them at once to the strongest possible individual case. Let us take the case of a murderer — the perpetrator of a crime needing the longest and strictest restraint; a profligate man, to whom the discipline needful for his improvement will seem most undesirable; a passionate and violent person, who will not shrink from committing a second murder to escape the consequences of the first; and one skilled by long practice in evasion of the law and its officers. Supposing that we had in readiness a place of secure restraint, physicians as eminently qualified to undertake the cure of depravity as the best to whom we now entrust friends otherwise diseased in mind or body, and all the appliances which the wealth of a nation can obtain, to carry on the course of treatment which these practitioners may indicate; the question still remains — HOW is such a man, against his will, to be arrested and subjected to this course of curative treatment, without injury to him, or the use of any means other than good and kind to overcome his evil?

How is his arrest effected, by the exercise of what qualities and instrumentalities, under our present system? Is it by any other than the use of courage, skill, and physical strength, backed by the use of deadly weapons? These are all! And all these are easily obtained, at a very moderate expense, and to whatever amount is thought needful by the government of any town or city. A skill, sufficient to circumvent the low cunning of the vicious classes, and a courage, ready to meet without flinching whatever peril to life or limb may be involved in conflict with the dangerous classes — these are common enough, and cheap enough; ready in the market at all times, in quantity more than sufficient to supply any demand that has yet arisen. True, as far as our experience has now gone, these qualities must be backed by the dirk and the revolver. *To these men*, this ultimate resort is indispensable. It is a very curious fact, that though the use of these "means of defence" (so they are termed) does not prevent their bearers from being shot, stabbed, killed on the spot — does not at all release them from the operation of the great law of God, that "Those who take the sword shall perish by the sword" — these men are ready, thus armed and accoutred, to risk their lives every day, and a dozen times a day, against superior force, similarly armed. The *courage* needful for this function, then, the readiness to encounter danger and death in the business of protecting society from malefactors, is common and easily obtained.

What qualities are needed to perform this indispensable work of arresting malefactors *in a manner accordant with Non-Resistance principles*, that is to say, accordant with the Christian law of love? Precisely those which we have already rehearsed, with a single exception. Courage, skill, and physical strength, *without* the use of deadly weapons. If these can be obtained, the greatest difficulty popularly supposed to interfere with the practical working of Non-Resistance (as far as the defence of a community from *internal* foes is concerned) is disposed of, and Non-Resistants may perfectly well, and with as great efficiency as is at present secured, perform the functions of a Police.

It is plain that animal courage, physical strength, and that acuteness of mind in meeting difficulties which, trained by practice, will produce skill, may be as certainly found among men of fixed good principle, as among men of no principle. These qualities are always in the market, always to be had where a sufficient price is offered for them, and they are to be had, conjoined with integrity, whenever this conjunction is demanded, and appropriate inducements offered for it. If the community really wished for such men as Isaac T. Hopper in the Police department, instead of such men as "Old Hays," it could have them. As yet, the demand has never existed.

A very great advantage (one which the prejudices of the community have thus far prevented them not only from realizing but from thinking of) might be gained from the employment of women with men, both in the care and instruction of criminals under restraint, and in the maintenance of public order as a police force. Women, with the grade of qualifications, natural and acquired, which I have assumed to be needed in men for these stations — women (such as we know) whose aspect shows at once the majesty of a noble character, the tenderness of a feeling heart, and the readiness to apply both to the relief of necessity or suffering — these would give immense assistance towards the great object of making authority persuasive, of refining, without weakening, the intercourse between the representative of law and the refractory subject of law. To give only one specification, what an immense difference would it make, both to the present and future of the poor vagrants of both sexes who go to the police station-houses for a night's lodging, if they could be received there by such a woman as Mrs. Garnaut was, and, after having their night made comfortable by her refined tenderness, have their morning brightened and their course directed by her judicious counsel and aid!

A few years ago, the inmates of a charitable institution in Boston found in one of their out-buildings, early in the morning, after a night of severe cold and deep snow, a woman, so benumbed as to be helpless, who had taken shelter there the preceding evening. The man nearest at hand to give help in carrying her into the house chanced to be an ex-policeman; and he said to the Matron — "I have often thought, Ma'am, that there ought to be women in the station-houses, where they often have to take care, for the night, not only of helpless women like this, but of drunken ones. Men ought not to have the handling of 'em. Women that are drunk are more violent and disorderly than men, and perhaps this wouldn't be so if they had their own sex to take care of 'em. It 's bad now, in many ways; and if there were respectable women there to see to things, they 'd make it much better, for all parties."

Nothing invigorates and fortifies a person in trying and dangerous circumstances so thoroughly as the consciousness of right. The consciousness of wrong, on the other hand, exercises a discouraging and depressing influence. This it is which gives to a police force their well known superiority over a gang of malefactors equal in number and strength to themselves, and armed with the same weapons. While their hearts are armed with this confidence, and their hands with deadly weapons, they do not hesitate at the habitual encounter with great risks, imminent dangers; neither are they deterred from these encounters by the fact that all their preparations do not insure them against bodily harm; the fact that from time to time they suffer wounds and bruises, and occasionally see their associates meeting a sudden and violent death, to which they know that they themselves are always exposed. It appears, then, that the voluntary and customary exposure of himself to danger and death is part of the regular business of a police officer, and that the actual realization of these possibilities, from time to time, does not deter men from assuming and executing this function. Let it be noted, that the Non-Resistant, who should undertake the preservation of order as a police officer, would have no greater and no other danger to encounter than this.

Those who have read the life of Isaac T. Hopper know that, in the numerous cases of aid which he rendered to fugitive slaves, he exposed himself to serious danger of bodily harm from slaveholders and kidnappers. He was not only not deterred by this danger from doing his intended work, but it seemed to be utterly disregarded by him. Of course, if his duty had required such action, he would no more have been prevented by danger from apprehending the kidnapper than from helping the slave.

Isaac T. Hopper was *successful* in a very great proportion

of the cases in which he interfered with slaveholders and kidnappers for the benefit of slaves; on these occasions, he met, and foiled, not only the class of persons just mentioned, but officers of the law; he foiled them by the use of their own weapons, strength, courage, confidence, stratagem, without the use of their auxiliary weapons of death; and he did all this at the disadvantage of acting in opposition to the law, bereft of that divinity which doth hedge an official personage, and of the great influence upon one's antagonist produced by acting with the law, and by express commission from the government.

Suppose we add to all the other high qualifications of such a man the advantage of a commission under the government, placing him openly on the side of the civil authorities, armed with the majesty of law, and authorized to call upon all well-disposed citizens for help in executing his function! Suppose we have Isaac T. Hopper enrolled among the police force, authorized to preserve order, quell disturbances, and arrest violators of the law! He understands this work, is competent to it, and thinks he can do it better without the use of sword or pistol, or even cane! Is there any thing to prevent his effective exercise of this function? Has he not the same inward consciousness of right that led him to face similar dangers for the deliverance of slaves? Has he not, in the legal commission, that same mighty moral power which now turns the scale in favor of the police force, when the malefactors are equal to them in numbers and weapons? Will his district of the city be more disorderly, will drunkards and brawlers bear sway there more than where a common policeman uses his accustomed methods of operation? Who believes it? We hazard nothing in saying that his function would be *more* effectively performed than that of others, in proportion to his mental and moral superiority.

Suppose, further, that this eminent man, so admirably qualified, both by his personal characteristics and by the respect of the whole population, to exercise the function of repressing disorder in the community, should have associates of similar character and qualities in this work. Suppose that a sense of the importance of cutting off, as far as possible, the sources of crime, should induce the community to select its very best, ablest, and noblest men to take charge of the execution of its penal laws — that is to say, of its reformatory system. Suppose that the whole police force (as well as the master and keepers of the reformatory establishments which would then have superseded our present jails) should be composed of men like Isaac T. Hopper; men without fear of injury to themselves — ready to encounter any danger in the discharge of the important function committed to them — determined to accomplish the work they have undertaken — determined to keep in mind the welfare of the criminal not less than of the community — and sustained in all this by the countenance, the thorough respect, (and the coöperation, in case of need,) of every well-disposed citizen. We are now prepared, I think, to undertake the solution of this hardest problem — to meet this extremest case, the fear of which now arms our police force with deadly weapons — namely, the arrest of an armed and desperate man.

It has not been sufficiently considered, in this matter, that the law and its officers are now often in the wrong, in some parts of their relation to the criminal, and that the criminal, in some respects, is wrongfully treated by them, and thus is, so far, on the right side in the controversy between them. For instance: all sorts of falsehood and treachery are freely used, by our present executive officers, to enable them to get possession of an alleged criminal; so that, when the final struggle comes, it is embittered by a keen desire for revenge, the criminal having been actually wronged, cheated and betrayed by the officer. This state of things very seriously interferes with the natural and proper relation of the two parties, and with the moral power that a representative of the law should have over a violator of the law. In the relation which I propose to establish between these parties, the criminal is to be in the wrong in every point, and the officer to be in the right in every point. No personal feeling against the executor of the law is to enforce the wish of the criminal to keep out of the hands of the law. On the contrary, the very aspect of our police officer is to display humanity not less than authority; the presence of love not less than the absence of fear; a genial, hearty good-will, which shall suggest the idea of trusting to him as a friend rather than of repelling him as an enemy; and an earnest uprightness, which shall agree with his well-known character, and assure the malefactor that he may thoroughly believe whatever that man says to him.

My own belief is that when a man like this, under circumstances like these, puts his hand on the shoulder of a criminal and says — "My friend, you must come with me!" — the criminal will find an unwonted difficulty in using his pistol or his bludgeon. In the first place, they are not needed! He has no personal violence, no bodily harm to fear, and no injury to avenge. He is talking with an unarmed man, a good and friendly man, a resolute and fearless man, a keen, acute and intelligent man, perfectly competent to the situation, and one who will be driven neither by threats nor violence from the performance of his duty. When this man thus accosts the criminal, one in the right in every particular of the relation between them, and speaking with the authority which that consciousness is fitted to impart, and at the same time arousing that consciousness in the breast of the criminal himself, I think the latter will not only feel himself more than ever before at disadvantage, but will, in the great majority of cases, feel himself defeated; I think there would be a quiet surrender in the majority of those cases which now are met by violent resistance.

But my business at present is to provide for the worst possible case; to suppose a man so resolute in his hardihood as to withstand all these influences, to refuse to surrender, and to undertake to escape capture by shooting dead on the spot even such a man as Isaac T. Hopper!

Does he escape capture by this means? Not at all! Our perfect police officer, who knows his man, and the situation, and the contingencies, has provided for this. He is ready to die in the discharge of his duty, but he has taken care that the work shall be performed, whether he dies or lives. At the sound of this murderous shot, two more men seize the criminal! two more of the same sort, and whom he knows to be of the same sort! Suppose the worst again, and that a second barrel of his revolver kills one of these! The third has him! The criminal has at once diminished his power and fearfully increased his guilt; and such of the community as are within sight or sound of the transaction, instead of giving unwilling and imperfect aid to an officer little better than the criminal, heartily and enthusiastically help the worthy representative of the majesty of the law. The criminal is seized, secured, and transported without injury to a place of safe restraint; and, from that time forward, whatever amount of uninjurious strength is needed to restrain him is ready for that purpose, and ready to meet whatever danger may be involved therein.

We have now the worst and most dangerous man in the community securely placed in the hands of the law. What is to be done with him?

Of course, this law, the execution of which, in its most perillous department, has been intrusted to Non-Resistants, will be in all respects, from beginning to end, of a Non-Resistance character. Being a law founded at once upon justice and upon love, it will be mindful of all the parties, and all the interests, committed to its charge.

The murderer has his trial, and is found guilty. What is to be done with him? He lies bound in the hands of the government, and they are to deal with him according to their best judgment, seeking to learn first, what is right, and then, among right things, which is best!

Let us turn aside a moment from this inquiry to look at the customary operation of our present penal laws, and see how near *they* come to what is right and what is best.

Our present law, assuming the intentional killing of a human being to be the greatest of crimes, allots to it this punishment — that the perpetrator be himself killed by a third person, in cold blood, at a specified time. It hopes thereby to accomplish these three purposes; to punish the criminal, to deter other criminals from murder, and to impress on the community a sense of "the sacredness of human life."

This community considers itself enlightened, civilized and Christian! Yet, in executing this important function of disposing of the murderer, it follows an old and barbarous Jewish law, which was explicitly revoked by the teacher whom the community pretends to follow; it disregards and violates the commands of that teacher, and the most characteristic feature of his system — the Christian system — namely, to forgive enemies, and to overcome evil with good; and it commits the unspeakable absurdity of deliberately destroying human life, "to show the sacredness of human life"! of deliberately killing a man, "to show the wickedness of killing men"!

The killing, thus ordered, is not, however, to be immediate. A certain interval of weeks or months is allowed the prisoner "to prepare for death," a work towards which numerous clergymen volunteer their aid. Before the end of this interval, it is usually announced that the criminal has been converted, and has become a Christian. His sins are forgiven! He is now "a child of God and an heir of heaven"! He has sincerely repented of his past offences, he is earnestly desirous to make reparation for them, as far as that is possible, and he shows so thoroughly the marks of a regenerate heart and a reformed character, that the Reverend clergy give him their highest certificate to this effect, admitting him to the communion of the Lord's Supper! He who was a profligate and a murderer is now a Christian! He has attained the grade to which his clerical advisers are vainly striving to bring the great mass of their congregations! He now belongs to the church, and is, like it, "the salt of the earth," "the light of the world."

What now, in these altered circumstances, is to be done with him? Just the same as before! He is to be killed in cold blood, "to vindicate the majesty of the law," and "to show the sacredness of human life"! Could any thing be more absurd — less Christian — more monstrous?

It is plain that here some improvement is possible! When the man whom we arrested and imprisoned because he was wicked and dangerous has become a good man, feeling in his own heart an utter unwillingness to do wrong, and a love of goodness for its own sake, we need his good influence in the community; we need his heart and hand in the work of applying Christianity to every-day life. We will restore him to society, both that he may repair, as far as possible, the particular injury of his former vicious course, and that he may help to Christianize the rest of the community, building again that which once he destroyed. This brings us to another particular of the ill working of the present system.

If, in the trial of the murderer, mitigating circumstances appear, or if the crime proved against him be of less enormity than murder, he is condemned, not to be killed, but to be imprisoned — as before, "to vindicate the majesty of the law." Of these cases, however, it is not found that the majority become Christianized, or otherwise reformed, during their incarceration. Some grow obviously worse, under the influences of the prison. Many, as obviously, receive no improvement from these influences. Both these classes, however, are discharged, "turned loose on the community," though with every prospect that they will commit new depredations upon it, when the term of their imprisonment arrives. So that it has become common for the keeper of a prison to expect that certain individuals of those whom he releases will shortly be returned to him, and to have that expectation realized. And hence, legislators as well as jailers have to make special provision for the cases of "second comers," "third comers," and "fourth comers." Here, at least, it is possible to make the improvement of *not* setting at large, to prey upon the community, persons more surely known to be wicked and dangerous than those who are newly arrested. If the community are right in keeping men under restraint at all, it would seem to be their duty and their interest to do these three things; to keep them under restraint as long as the reasons for doing so remain in equal force, to apply all the means in their power to the removal of those reasons, and to release the prisoners when there is good reason to suppose that they will be good instead of evil members of society.

Let us glance at another great defect and evil of our present system. The arrest of a malefactor in many cases takes away the means of sustenance of his family. His wife and children, who are likely already to have become contaminated by evil company, and to have fallen under the power of vicious habits, are left entirely unregarded by the community. They may be in extreme want, or in the very worst conditions for their social, mental, moral and religious welfare! Is this right? Ought not the children at least to receive a care, supplying the place of that which their father was accustomed to give, and which the State has prevented him from giving? And, in so far as his care was insufficient, or positively detrimental to them, should not the State seize eagerly the opportunity of supplying a better? The children of the incarcerated criminal should of course be taken from influences tending to make *them* criminal, and should have the benefit of proper sustenance and good instruction. Would not Isaac T. Hopper and his associates rejoice to perform this function?

Would not the government which had selected such men for its officers of course authorize and require them to do this? A Non-Resistant government would never leave a large class of children to grow up criminals for want of proper instruction and care!

The wife of the imprisoned criminal may be unable to support herself at all, or may have experienced great difficulties in finding an honest support. A good government should provide that its citizens be not driven by want into crime. A Non-Resistant government would take special care that its justice to the husband did not operate cruelly and unjustly upon the wife. And the administration which was wise enough to choose Isaac T. Hopper among its police would already have commissioned John Augustus or Mrs. Garnaut to look after the necessities of the wife, and Charles F. Barnard to provide for the children, while it committed the dangerous husband and father to a house of reformation directed by Dr. Follen, Horace Mann, or Dr. Howe.

Those who have the care of lunatic Asylums have to contend against the very utmost exertions of bodily strength, often directed by a craft which seems preternatural in its acuteness. They are not vanquished by these difficulties; on the contrary, they overcome them, and by the use of judicious and humane, not brutal, instrumentalities. They not only obtain a systematic control over these most unpromising of subjects, but they restore to reason such of them as are susceptible of cure, simply by unwearied persistence in the right method; and this in spite of the fact that we have not, in the management of insane Asylums, men so lofty in genius or so replete with intelligence and skill as the persons whom we have supposed to be placed in charge of the reformation of criminals. The same amount of skill and perseverance would accomplish at least as much with men diseased in the moral department. We need, for this most refractory class of pupils, the very highest capacity, intellectual, moral, religious, administrative, that exists in the community. The greatness of the end in view not only justifies, but demands, that the very highest wisdom, excellence and skill that the community affords shall be sought for this purpose, and obtained for it, at whatever expense may be needful. For the ultimate object is the extirpation of crime from the community, and the immediate object is the rapid progressive diminution of crime, as far as these can be accomplished by municipal and educational arrangements.

It is an enormous blunder to assume that those things *cannot* be done which have never yet been attempted. Yet the community are constantly making this blunder.

A Non-Resistance government would do these three things, which no existing government has ever even undertaken:

It would take care, and most vigilant and judicious care, of all children and youth who were neglected by their natural guardians. This alone would diminish by nine-tenths the next generation of criminals. It is an unspeakable disgrace to the States, cities and towns of New England, that no such thing is even attempted by them.

It would apply itself vigorously to the suppression and removal of the most obvious public nurseries and stimulants of crime. The police of every city know perfectly well the grog-shops, the gambling-rooms, the houses of assignation and prostitution, and the customary frequenters of all these, as well as the pickpockets and burglars. Yet they let them pursue their course of devastation, merely tything, as it were, the harvest of criminals which they produce. If the courage, the skill, the energy and the perseverance of Isaac T. Hopper were commissioned by the government to suppress these, and put an end to them, would not a progress, in geometrical ratio, be annually made towards this end? Now, it is not even attempted.

Thirdly, a Non-Resistance government, having put under restraint a man who was dangerous to the community, would apply all the means in its power to the work of transforming him into a good man and a useful citizen, and would keep him under restraint until he had ceased to be dangerous. In their reformatory institution, the "second comers" (if there were *any* such) would diminish, from year to year, in a geometrical ratio. As a general rule, from the moment a criminal came into the hands of the police, he might be considered as a reformed man, as far as any further depredations on the community were concerned.

Is this a very great, a very difficult undertaking? It is on account of my conviction that it is so that I demand the very highest ability and excellence in the community, not only to superintend this work, but to perform all its details. When these are secured, the work will necessarily go on, with no more obstruction to its successful progress than the occasional unruliness of a horse gives to the movements of a mail coach.

But the laws must be altered, to allow either the detention of a prisoner until he is reformed, or his discharge as soon as he is reformed!

No doubt. Our laws need many changes to bring them in correspondence with justice, and with public and private welfare. But let us have those changes.

Many prisons, many lunatic Asylums, are now conducted not only with humanity, but with a fair measure of success, in proportion to their moderate aspirations and their moderate instrumentalities. When, instead of prisons, we have Houses of Reformation, all the regulations, arrangements, implements and functionaries of which are adapted, with special care and skill, to promote the real welfare of the prisoner, and to prove, *to his apprehension*, that such is their meaning and purpose, it is not too much to say that we may confidently expect success, in no long period, in the great majority of instances. If criminals have hitherto shown themselves stubborn in regard to the two sorts of influence commonly brought to bear upon them, a hard, worldly keenness, backed by physical force, in which they find no human sympathy, or a pious verdancy which every smart rogue feels that he can wind round his finger, this is no reason why they should not yield to the system devised and administered by Dr. Follen or Horace Mann.

Bring forward your extreme case, your "tough subject," your "fourth comer" to the State Prison, the man who has run the gauntlet of all the penal institutions, and who is at once recognized as irreclaimable by them all, in short, the man who, having been arrested for murder by Isaac T. Hopper, has shot him dead on the spot, has also killed on the spot his first assistant, and then has been secured, without injury to himself, and brought within the walls of our true House of Reformation.

He escaped from the persuasive magnetism of Isaac T. Hopper's face, eye and voice, by killing him. He has now no weapon. He is disarmed and securely bound. He *must* see, he *must* hear, he *must* feel the controlling influence of those with whom he has now to do.

He finds these characteristics in the Governor of the establishment, and *also in the particular person to whose charge he is committed*, namely: —

1. An overwhelming superiority in character, intelligence, skill, tact, insight, energy, moral power. He feels that these men are "masters of the situation"! That they understand him, even *comprehend* him, while he can neither comprehend nor understand them. He feels, at once, the thorough hopelessness of any hypocritical pretence with them; feels himself transparent before their gaze, and incapable of any plan which shall deceive them. He is compelled to admire and respect their knowledge and skill.

2. He sees with this, and just as obviously, in the faces of these men, a genial, friendly nature; a sympathy, human and humane, so abiding and controlling, so broad and so deep, that he feels even himself, the murderer, the baffled, convicted and subdued criminal, to be comprehended in it. These are men whom he would be glad to have, if he could, for friends.

3. When the purpose and method of the establishment, and the particular details of his position in it are made known to him, he must see, because it shines conspicuously through all the arrangements, that these are not an apparatus of vengeance, but of benefit, and that his real welfare is contemplated and provided for in it, not less than the welfare of the community.

4. When he comes to receive instruction, — not the Sunday school lesson, given by some well-meaning sectarian whose shallowness is displayed in every question and every exhortation, but real food for the mind and soul, given by a person as distinguished in character and attainments as we have endeavored to describe — when he comes to receive suggestions and ideas from one who thoroughly understands him, under stands his capacities, his deficiencies, his possibilities, the right way to approach him, the things he may be led to desire, the desires he is competent to achieve — and when (sooner or later) he clearly recognizes this union of competence and friendliness in his teacher, who shall say that even this man, hardened and desperate as he seemed, may not be brought to recognize his own manhood, with its inseparable duties and responsibilities! his duties to God, with the fact, resulting from God's very nature, that He helps those who help them-

selves! and his duties to his injured fellow-men, with the assurance that it is never too late to repent, and to bring forth fruits meet for repentance! Who shall say that even this man, thus situated and thus influenced, every where encouraged by the friendly aid of superior beings, every where assisted to aspire and to attain, having nothing to hope but from a right course, having every thing to hope from earnest amendment and strenuous endeavor, will not heartily coöperate with these beneficent influences, work out through them his enfranchisement, and become a blessing to that community from which he was taken as a curse?

If *this* man shall first yield to, and then spontaneously and heartily unite in, means of correction and development such as we have described, who shall withstand them?

If, on the other hand, he, with the most hardened of his fellow-criminals, shall remain unconverted and unreformed, still, will not this class probably be a very small one — *much* smaller than the proportion of unreclaimed offenders in our present civilization?

At all events, the system I propose will have these very great advantages over the present one. It will *tend*, constantly, and strongly, towards the real reformation of every criminal under its jurisdiction; and the convicts who remain unreformed will remain in custody, with no power any further, or in any manner, to injure the community.

Let me briefly rehearse the things which I have attempted to show in the foregoing pages: —

1. The system called (for shortness) "Non-Resistance," is not an inert and merely harmless thing, but it proposes to execute the two duties expressed in the Christian precept — "Overcome evil with good." It purposes constant aggression against evil and sin, and also to conduct this aggression invariably by right means. It purposes to *overcome* evil; it is equally resolute to overcome it *with good.*

2. As an individual may lead a life of thorough conformity to Non-Resistance principles, avoiding injury to others, forgiving injury done to himself, and overcoming evil with good, however circumstances may involve him with criminals and ruffians, so a community may do these things, conduct its affairs on these same principles, and require its official ser-

vants, from the highest to the lowest, to act in accordance with them.

3. As insane people, including both the most crafty and the most violent, are put under restraint, kept under restraint, and subjected to whatever beneficial discipline is thought desirable for their welfare, without wounding or killing them, so can the violators of law be apprehended, and subjected to needful restraint and discipline, without wounding or killing *them*. The superintendent, physician and functionaries of an insane Asylum are expected to do their work without injuring their patients, and they *do* it. Those who have charge of the arrest and the discipline of criminals can do the same thing, if it is required of them.

4. The moral power which officers of government possess in being on the side of law, and commissioned by the community to preserve order, already great, may be indefinitely increased by giving the discharge of the executive functions to men already respected for eminent ability and distinguished excellence of character.

5. The moral power of the law, already great, may be immensely increased by bringing all its methods of administration into conformity with justice, with the *rights* of all, even of the criminal, and with the *welfare* of all, even of the criminal.

6. Duty and interest alike require that the community should use all possible means for the reformation and improvement of those whom they hold under restraint, as dangerous; that the restraint begun for this reason should be continued as long as needed; and that it should cease when it ceases to be needed.

7. Duty and interest alike require that the State should take under its charge children and youth who are deprived of or neglected by their natural guardians; especially those children whose guardians have been removed from them by the State.

8. The great advantages which may reasonably be expected from a system like the above — namely, the increase of efficiency in the administration of law resulting from the increased moral power of its ministers and modes of operation, and the progressive diminution of crime certain to result from a substitution of reformatory discipline for vindictive punish-

ment — not only justify and recommend, but most strongly encourage, the employment of the very best and ablest men and women in the community in these departments.

In showing how the *arrest* of the criminal may be effected by the use of means uninjurious to him, I have shown how *all* those departments of a just government which deal with criminals may be carried on by Non-Resistants, upon Non-Resistance principles. For, of course, the same methods would be used to suppress a popular tumult or riot, namely, a fearless and prompt interposition of the physical strength and the moral power of the police (who would, if necessary, call the community to their aid) between the rioters and their unlawful purpose. If, at first, fear were entertained in regard to the efficiency of officers acting without deadly weapons, either in dealing with individual criminals or with a mob, their number could be increased; could be doubled, trebled or quadrupled, at the commencement of a trial of the new method; or could receive a partial trial, (with the precaution last named, if that were thought needful,) in certain specified districts of a town or city. But it is obvious that, after the establishment and the general recognition of the system proposed, the character of the officers of justice would insure the giving of whatever personal aid might be required, by the community around, far more generally and more heartily than at present.

www.ingramcontent.com/pod-product-compliance
Lightning Source LLC
LaVergne TN
LVHW011138110826
845150LV00008B/2401